CBD OIL
INDIANA'S ROAD TO
MARIJUANA

RUDY KACHMANN, M.D.

Published by Rudy Kachmann, M.D.

All rights reserved. No part of this publication may be reproduced or transmitted in any form or by any means, electronic or mechanical, including photocopying and recording, or by any information storage and retrieval system, without permission from the publisher and copyright owners.

ISBN: 978-1-791-76506-4

Printed in the United States of America.

Contents

Preface 1

Cannabis in History 3

The Marijuana Plant 7

The Endocannabinoid System 9

The Cytochrome P450 System (CYP) 13

The Main Lie: Marijuana is Not Harmful 17

Our Children Are Going to Pot 21

Harming and Killing Our Children by Allowing Them to Vape 29

What about the Placebo Effect? 33

State and Local Laws Regarding Medical Marijuana 37

The Colorado Experience 43

What the Indiana legislature Could Learn from Colorado, California, Oregon and the State of Washington 49

Two False Beliefs 53

Medical Marijuana 59

Methods of Using Medical Cannabis 63

Medical Marijuana Side Effects 65

Legalization of Marijuana Can Lead to Other Problems 67

The Entourage Effect: Drug Interaction 69

Combining Alcohol and CBD Oil Can Be Deadly 73

Appreciate a Second Opinion 75

Summary: The Road to Marijuana 77

References 81

Preface

This book was written to encourage you to expand your knowledge about the cannabis plant and its main chemicals, marijuana, and CBD.
The Indiana Legislature and governor this year signed into law rules that say you can sell and buy CBD products at retail businesses, with no age requirement and no warnings about possible interactions or side effects.

Health food stores, chiropractors, doctors, nurses, physician assistants, gas stations, physical fitness businesses—all types of retail shops are selling it. I checked five retail businesses who sell the product, and no one asked if I was on any other medications. My biggest concern has been that CBD products can turn off a significant set of liver enzymes that detoxify our bodies of the medications and supplements we are already taking. I asked 10 people who are on CBD products at a well-known fitness business, and no one knew that those pharmaceuticals they're on could become more potent or less effective. There are many other dangers from using CBD and marijuana and I will discuss those further in this book.

I welcome a discussion. I don't have any agenda. I'm just trying to open the door to knowledge. I will list a lot of references in case you want to read further. I encourage you to go online, because a lot of information is available there on this subject. I will discuss the experience of other states, especially

Colorado and some others. That information is available to you also on the internet.

Our government passed this legislation on CBD without informing us of the potential problems. They should've required that all the products be labeled with further information on its interaction with heat, as well as what it does to our lungs and livers. Especially concerning are the effects they have on our children. They can even cause permanent brain damage.

Now, e-cigarettes and vaping are exploding in our schools. That's the last thing we needed. What's even worse is that children are heating CBD, which can partially convert it to THC. The information on how to do it can be easily obtained online.

We the people need to stand up and stop this train before it's left the station. That's what I am trying to do. This book will help give you knowledge and references for your own use to help you communicate with your politicians. Please join me in this effort. Some of this information will shock you because it is hard to understand how our government could possibly do this to us. The government, industry, and politicians think they're going to make a lot of money. What happens to the rest of us does not matter to them. Please join me on this march to stop this train of greedy people. I think you will have some motivation after reading this book.

Cannabis in History

Cannabis seeds where excavated in burial mounds in Siberia. They date back to 3000 BC. Large amounts of mummified marijuana were also found in the tombs of aristocrats in China, going back to around 2500 BC.

The use of marijuana then spread to neighboring Korea around 2000 BC, and from there to the South Asian region, including India, in around 1500 BC.

The earliest mention of the use of cannabis in the Western world was around 440 BC. They were using it in steam baths and deriving great pleasure from the effects. This appears to be the beginning of recreational use of the plant. The Greeks and Romans also used marijuana and hemp for recreational and industrial purposes. They used it for ropes and sails. The Muslims in north Africa used the word "hashish" or hash, referring to smoke from marijuana and literally meaning "dry weed." With the spread of the Islamic empire, cannabis use expanded to the Western Hemisphere, mainly through the wide-ranging exploration of the Spaniards in various parts of the world. By the 1500s, cannabis was already extensively grown in both North and South America.

While the leaves and flowers of the hemp plant are used to produce pot, these and other parts including stems, roots, and seeds can also be used to make hemp fiber, building materials, and textiles.

Another product of the plant is hemp oil, which can be consumed as food or made into an ingredient in lotions, cosmetics, and other body care products. Perhaps the most valuable role the hemp plant served was for medicinal purposes. Hemp has in fact been singled out as the only plant that contains all of the essential amino acids and fatty acids needed by the human body. Many rugs, nets, sails, and ship riggings are made from hemp.

As a fuel, hemp oil was traditionally used to light lamps. Petroleum largely replaced it in the late 1800s. As building materials, hemp products were used much like wood to build homes and structures.

As an illicit drug, marijuana is often smoked in hand rolled cigarettes called joints. You can also smoke it in the form of blunts. Marijuana cigars are made by cutting regular cigars open and replacing the tobacco inside with weed. Marijuana can also be consumed by mouth, as when it is mixed with certain foods such as cookies, candies, and brownies.

Over the years, many strains of cannabis have been developed and bred to suit any of the specific purposes discussed above. Some cannabis strains produce abundant fiber, others CBD, and mainly THC plants.

In 1450 BC, mention is made of the substance in the book of Exodus as a "Holy anointing oil." In 1213 BC, Egyptian healers used cannabis to cure inflammation and gout. And it was also used when administering enemas.

In 600 BC, marijuana appears in Indian medical literature as a cure for leprosy. In 70 AD, it was used by Roman doctors medicinally to cure ear aches. In the 1600s, the famous English poet William Shakespeare may have smoked marijuana. A number of pipes, joints, and stems allegedly belonging to him were recovered and forensically examined. Between 1745 and 1775, the future US president George Washington grew hemp on his plantation at Mount Vernon. He was deeply interested in the medicinal uses of the plant, and probably used it recreationally too, as his diaries revealed. In the late 1700s, the French Emperor Napoleon invaded Egypt and brought to the country a scientific expedition team. They brought cannabis back with them when they returned to France in 1799, but then Napoleon outlawed its use among his army. In 1842, the famous Irish doctor William O'Shaughnessy reintroduced marijuana into British medicine when he got back from his stint as an army surgeon in British-controlled India. In 1911, Massachusetts became the first state in the US to officially declare cannabis a dangerous drug and ban its use. From 1913 to 1917, other states followed the example of Massachusetts and declared cannabis illegal.

The Marijuana Plant

Cannabis is the genus name, and sativa, indica, and rubialis are the main species names.

Tetrahydrocannabinol (THC) and Cannabinodiol (CBD) are extracted from the marijuana plant. There is more THC in the indica plant, and more CBD in the sativa plant. They are cultivated in many parts of the world for industrial hemp, which has been used for ropes and sales for thousands of years. It can also be a source of medicinal and recreational marijuana as well. Cannabis Indica is primarily used to produce recreational and medicinal marijuana, and it's not used for industrial hemp, because of its poor fiber quality.

Cannabis has leaves, flowers, stems, and roots. Its leaves consist of anywhere from one to thirteen leaflets. When you grow it in the wild, the hemp plant has very long roots that are about as long as the part of the plant that is above ground. Cannabis cultivated by people has a much shorter root system. That is because the soil used by private or commercial growers is usually more nutrient-dense than the soil in the wild.

When the leaves, flowers, and flower buds of the hemp plant are dried and shredded, the resulting grayish-green or brownish-green mixture is called marijuana. It goes by many different names: pot, grass, weed, herb, Mary Jane, hash, refried, ham, boom, gangster, dog, etc.

Marijuana can be smoked or inhaled, drunk like tea, or eaten—as when mixed with brownies, cookies, and other foods. It has an intoxicating effect, producing a high that can be addictive. It is classified as a controlled substance, and its recreational use is illegal in many states. It is illegal according to a federal law. We will discuss this further in another chapter. The stems and roots are primarily used to make hemp fiber and oil. Hemp fiber is also used to make fabrics, such as canvas, rock, paper, textiles, and fuel oil. Hemp seed and hemp oil are also used as food and dietary supplements.

The plants grow best in humid and tropical places, but you can grow it in most climates. You can grow it anywhere in the world, because they can be cultivated indoors in a controlled environment. Some people grow it indoors or in private yards to avoid detection, because it is illegal to cultivate in many parts of the world, including many states in United States

The Endocannabinoid System

The ECS: it's like several other neuro-modulatory systems in our bodies, like the quick-fix system dopamine, including the nucleus accumbens in our posterior frontal lobe, which makes us feel good immediately after eating sugar, smoking a cigarette, having a drink, smoking a joint, laughing, dancing, or exercising.

The ECS was discovered in rats around 1990. It is involved with a variety of physiological processes, including appetite, pain sensation, memory, gastrointestinal functions, inflammatory responses, and immune function. Unfortunately, the NIH at the time supported research to prove the deleterious effects of cannabis, while blocking research into the beneficial effects. Therefore, the science has been lagging. For example, we generally don't hear about how CBD, medical marijuana, and marijuana itself are metabolized.

The ECS is like the dopamine, serotonin, and adrenergic pathways in the body. It is comprised of at least three neuromodulators and at least two receptors, CB1 and CB2. These receptors are found in the brain and body, especially in the immune system.

The Entourage Effect refers to the synergistic influence on these modulating factors which occurs when several of the related cannabinoids are present at one time, as opposed to the effects when just one isolated cannabinoid is present at their receptors. That is why I am concerned about the tests that have been run on the products being sold at retail stores. It is estimated that the testing of the products sold, which are done by whatever company sells the product, runs at only a 26% accuracy rate.

The CB1 receptors are mainly in the brain, cerebellum, hippocampus, and brainstem. There are some in the body also. The CB2 receptors are mainly in the body, including the arms and legs, heart, and immune system. It is believed the ECS plays a vital role and modulating transmitter release to maintain homeostasis and in preventing excessive neuronal activity. There is good evidence that the ECS receptors can inhibit or excite any ongoing release of a number of different excitatory and inhibitory new transmitters, including acetylcholine, dopamine, noradrenaline, GABA, and 5-HT.

CB1 and CB2 receptors respond to the endocannabinoids naturally produced by the body, to phytocannabinoids from the cannabis plant, and to the newer synthetic cannabinoids developed by pharmaceutical companies. There has been increased interest in CBD, but actually it bears little affinity for either receptor. Instead, it suppresses AEA and 2-AG activity.

Cannabinoid receptor-1 and CB1 are present in varying degrees in several structures within the brain, including the amygdala, which regulates anxiety and fear, the basal ganglia, which regulates reaction time, the brainstem, which regulates nausea effects, the cerebellum, which regulates coordination and balance, the hippocampus, which regulates short-term memory, the hypothalamus, which is involved in appetite and sexual behavior, and temperature, the neocortex, which is involved in complex thinking and judgment, the nucleus accumbens, which regulates rewards and pleasure sensations, and the spinal cord, which regulates pain perception. CB1 receptor cells are present in these areas as well, but to a much lesser extent. They are also found in the uterus, pancreas, liver, gastrointestinal tract, and in adipose (fat) tissue. CB1 regulates psychoactive, central nervous system, and some anticonvulsive affects.

THE ENDOCANNABINOID SYSTEM

CB2 receptors are found on leukocytes and throughout the body in the immune system, spleen, and throughout the nervous system. They are likewise present to some extent throughout our second brain—the gut.

In the immune system, the ECS modulates cytokine production, immune cell migration, and apoptosis. In most cells, CB2 receptors modulate inflammatory response. In the GI tract, activation of CB2 receptors results in regulation of intestinal motility, and smooth muscle contractions in the urinary and reproductive systems. AEA, our own principle endocannabinoid, stimulates the CB1 receptors in the brain. In the periphery, it is also a CB2 stimulator.

The current research suggests that hypothalamic neurons continually produce endocannabinoids that work to regulate hunger. It also suggests that the cannabinoid activity in the brain is strongly related to food-seeking behavior.

What I have tried to describe is a complex system that can help us or harm us when we try to stimulate it with an exogenous plant chemical like cannabinoids, CBD, or THC. We are not knowledgeable about the detoxification of these chemicals. We have legalized the sale of CBD but not told the public about the metabolic pathways it affects. CBD turns off some of the Cytochrome P450 metabolic pathway, especially if the person is taking in the cannabinol product when they are already on a number of other medications. You can buy the product without a prescription and personally I think that can be harmful and deadly. I am relaying the science to you in this book.

The Cytochrome P450 System (CYP)

CBD or THC, along with the rest of the cannabinoids they contain, will eventually have to be metabolized by the gut, liver, and occasionally other parts of the body. The cytochrome system, abbreviated CYP, is the most important system involved with cannabis metabolism. It accounts for 75% of the enzymes involved with medication metabolism in general.

There are 60 CYP genes; however, only a few are tested for when prescribing cannabis. What concerns me a great deal is that people are buying cannabis products like CBD without age restriction and have no idea that they have the chemical power to turn off the metabolizer of many of the medications they're taking.

CYP enzymes are involved with catalyzing, upgrading, or downgrading a vast number of reactions, mostly in the liver. CYP can detoxify medicinal compounds to facilitate excretion or turn inactive compounds into active pharmacological agents.

For example, if CYP enzymes metabolize a drug slowly, the drug stays longer in the body. If it metabolizes a drug more quickly, a higher dose may be needed to have an effect. Many medications in other substances, such as alcohol, can lead to synthesis of other CYP enzymes, making it more metabolically active.

You can see if someone is going to take CBD products, they would need to be going to a physician who is highly trained in the pharmacology of drug interactions. But that will not happen in today's free-for-all of buying CBD products. I doubt there will be a medical provider at the gas station.

There are several CYP enzymes that can be tested for prior to use of cannabinoids. The first one is CYP2D6. This enzyme acts on 25% of all known drugs, including cannabinoids. As you already know, this would only occur in very rare situations. The law signed by the Indiana House, Senate, and Governor's office did not include mandatory testing for people who are taking other medications. A wide variety of medications, as well as grapefruit juice and CBD products, work as strong inhibitors of the P450 enzyme, which may amplify or weaken their response to the drugs the patient is already taking. Sorry that I keep on repeating that, but it may help you avoid complications— or even death.

The extent to which CBD behaves as a competitive inhibitor of Cytochrome P450 depends on how and how much CBD is administered. Every person responds differently, and it can be a serious problem even when they are not on multiple other medications. This means that patients ingesting CBD products should pay close attention to changes in the blood levels of important drugs they are taking and adjust accordingly under a doctor's supervision. Again, I doubt they will have a supervising physician when buying it from non-pharmacies.

Suppose a patient is taking chemotherapy and CBD. The same dose of chemotherapy may produce high blood concentrations of the chemo drugs, and that could be fatal and not effective. The same thing could happen with an epilepsy patient. The interaction would change the effectiveness of the seizure medication.

Evidence suggests that CBD can either increase or decrease the breakdown of other drugs, depending on the drug and the dosages used. The references for that statement are on page 73 of the book called *CBD* by

THE CYTOCHROME P450 SYSTEM (CYP)

Leonard Leinow and Juliana Birnbow, which is incidentally a great book to read about CBD.

Drug interactions are especially important to consider when using life-saving drugs, drugs with narrow therapeutic windows, or medications with major adverse side effects.

The list below does not necessarily contain every medication that could be affected by CBD, and not every medication in each of the categories listed in the book causes the interaction. For this reason, don't take CBD as an alternative medication, or dosage adjustments will be needed. I don't know what our governor and legislature were thinking when they passed the law without considering the above information. I will list some of the drugs that use the Cytochrome P450 System. As already stated, this is only a partial list:

- Steroids
- HMG CoA reductase inhibitors
- Calcium channel blockers
- Antihistamines
- Pro kinetics
- HIV antivirals
- Immune modulators
- Benzodiazepines
- Anti-arrhythmias
- Antibiotics
- Anesthetics
- Antipsychotics
- Antidepressants
- Antiepileptics
- Beta blockers
- PPIs
- NSAIDs
- Angiotensin II blockers
- Oral hypoglycemic agents

- Sulfonylureas

One's total body makeup is a moving target, and attempts at cannabis therapy without clear indications, which are very few, without an expert physician, can be very dangerous. Although it is always a good idea to consult a doctor for diagnosis and guidance, the fact is that very few practitioners are skilled in the nuances of cannabis therapy, strain selection, CBD ratio selection, and dosage guidance. In addition, each person has a distinct body weight and chemistry as well as unique sensitivity or tolerance to cannabinol products like CBD.

The Main Lie: Marijuana is Not Harmful

About 12% of Americans are addicted to alcohol, about 9% of adults are addicted to marijuana, and 17% of adolescents will develop an addiction to marijuana.

Such problems are much more likely to arise if someone uses marijuana daily or nearly every day, or if someone begins regular use as an adolescent. Occasional marijuana use is less likely to be harmful in the same way that drinking in moderation in some people does not seem to lead to habituation or addiction. But people smoking multiple times a week usually leads to regular use. Daily or near daily use often leads to marijuana addiction, as already mentioned. The Diagnostic and Statistical Manual of Mental Health Disorders (DSM-5) details how Marijuana Use Disorder often causes major problems in many important areas of a person's life, such as school, work, or relationships. Right now, about 2.7 million Americans are addicted to marijuana—and could benefit from treatment.

But rather than tackling this issue, state legislatures in places like Indiana are promoting medical marijuana in various guises, including CBD oils.

The political push will be hard to fight. Major government and corporate leaders are backing leading marijuana companies to make a lot of money.

Especially, with Canada legalizing marijuana, it will be difficult to resist changes in our national laws. It's the money.

Catastrophic events, overdoses, assaults, and the rest are what often lead people into treatment for the "hard drugs." They may say no one ever overdosed on marijuana, but I don't agree. Marijuana and CBD can be the cause of medical harm or death through the inactivation, at least in part, of the Cytochrome P450 enzymes.

I do some teaching and wellness coaching at major factories, and about 70% of the workers I meet smoke cigarettes. One of these workers once said to me, "You realize Doc, a significant number of the people here are also smoking marijuana." The company actually has a policy of unannounced drug testing, which means some workers are going to lose their jobs. The reason is that while alcohol and opiates are detoxified in a matter of hours, it takes days or weeks to detoxify cannabinoids. Many would lose their employment, and job terminations involve walking you out the door. Worse, other companies may not hire you because of your history of testing positive for illicit substances.

Scientific research shows that regular marijuana use affects the ability to think, can increase feelings or anxiety and depression, and can likewise increase the odds that one will develop psychotic disorders such as schizophrenia.

Your brain cannot perform the way it's supposed to when you use marijuana. The main active ingredient in the drug is THC, which produces the high. When you heat CBD, you can convert some of that into THC. The method is readily available on the internet. So, we can easily see how dangerous it is to sell CBD across our state, without age restriction, without warnings about how it is metabolized and interacts with the medications you're already taking.

The potency of the products sold has increased tremendously in the last 10 years, making them still more dangerous. THC affects your body by plugging into the microscopic sockets in the brain called "cannabinoid receptors." Many of these receptors are found in the parts of the brain that control thinking, concentration, coordination, and memory. The short-term effects of marijuana use include increased heart rate, slow reaction time, car accidents, and balance problems with increased falls.

The long-term effects of regular marijuana use are even more troublesome. Regular marijuana use hinders frontal-executive brain function, the ability to perform tasks that require complex thinking. For example, suppose you're riding a bicycle or motorcycle, and you have smoked marijuana in the last hour: your judgment will be severely impaired, as well as your balance.

Those who began smoking marijuana regularly before age 16 perform especially poorly on cognitive tests. Marijuana use at any age can cause serious problems but use among those age 16 or younger is especially worrisome, because of the increased likelihood of addiction and the potential long-term consequences on brain development. The results have been demonstrated in functional MRI scans. I have personally reviewed them. The holes in the brain do not repair themselves. You can take a brilliant child and convert her to an average child. You can take an average child and convert him to a below-average child.

Studies have even shown that regular marijuana use causes your IQ to drop. A recent study by Duke University followed more than 1000 New Zealand residents over their lifetimes, measuring their scores on IQ tests at ages 13 and 38. This proves that regular marijuana use beginning in the teenage years leads to a decline in IQ. Those who use marijuana regularly for years experience about an 8-point drop in their IQ scores over a 25-year period. The science is out there, and we have to accept that before passing legislation that legalizes cannabinol products.

Our Children Are Going to Pot

We have about 25 million people who are addicted to a substance like opioids or marijuana. For about 20 million of them, it's actually the latter.

So, when we say that 80% of the people addicted to opioids started with a doctor's prescription, that's blatantly wrong. Eighty percent of them may have been on a doctor's prescription early on and became addicted for life, but marijuana was often there first. Yet, hardly anybody ever brings that up. I recently reviewed many scientific papers and at least five books about opioids and marijuana. There's no question in my mind about the role of weed.

At this time, about 9% of adults are addicted to cannabinoids, the chemicals in marijuana, about 17% of children. Twenty-four percent of smokers began in adolescence. The rate keeps on rising because of increased availability and reduced restrictions on purchases.

I have reviewed an excellent book written by William J. Bennett, who had been the drugs czar under President George H.W. Bush. Under Ronald Reagan, he had been the Head of the Department of Education. I would say being the drugs czar is great credentials. The name of the book is *Going to Pot*. I've read it about three times and check out many of his references. I used to think that physicians' prescriptions were the biggest cause of our "Addict

Nation". I'm now convinced it's our rate of marijuana smoking, which starts for many in childhood.

Throughout these chapters, I will discuss the effects of the 700 chemicals that are in marijuana on the human body. It causes short-term memory loss in children and adults. Because the child's brain is still developing till about age 25, it actually causes brain damage, which has been proven by autopsies and functional MRI scans. The proof is there. Unfortunately, that's not reversible, and it makes it difficult for these children to learn and retain information. Our memories are built for taking in information, storing it, organizing it, and then expressing it in a logical form when called for. Can you imagine what that will do to the child's future, or to an adult at work?

Cannabinoids also impair motor coordination, while driving, working, at home, playing sports, or during any other activity. Falls are common. As a matter fact, a fall is the most common source of trauma for humans. The emergency room doctors told me that. In the states allowing marijuana shops, injuries and mortality from car accidents have increased significantly.

THC, the main active chemical in marijuana, causes altered judgment, increased risk of unprotected sexual behavior, causing transmission of sexual diseases and unintended pregnancies. You can see the problems that would cause. How about the effects on that child born from an addicted mother—or even a casual marijuana user?

Researchers have also found that marijuana use increases rates of paranoia and psychosis. At least 10% of psychotics have been found to be users.

The federal government has never done clinical trials on the interaction of THC and most medications people might be taking. They could potentially interact with each other, causing mortalities, accidental or intentional.

Again, long-term use leads to about a 90% addiction rate. That occurs in around 17% of people who started use in adolescence, and in 25-50% in daily users.

Long-term users have altered brain development, generally a poor educational outcome, and increased rates of dropping out of the school. The average cognitive impairment results in a decrease in IQ of about 9%. Most have diminished life satisfaction and achievement.

In long term users, and sometimes even short-term ones, researchers are also finding cardiovascular effects. Some children are having strokes and unexpected heart attacks from marijuana use. There have been increased rates of bronchitis and asthma as well. If your child is coughing all the time and you can't figure out why, keep your eyes open.

Something the promoters of marijuana use don't bring up is the great increase in potency of what they're selling now—especially in the states that have completely approved its use. Of course, unexpected complications and even deaths have occurred because of that, especially when it's first-time users visiting other states that have marijuana shops. The Colorado ski resorts for example have found that 90% of the marijuana sold there is to out-of-state residents. A significant number have never tried it before—don't you expect that some fell off the mountain when attempting to ski? I know of people who have moved to that state because of the availability of cannabinoids. What do you think? Do some bring it home? Do you think some of them might even be selling it here?

The federal government still has laws against the selling or use of marijuana. They just don't enforce the law. That's a horrible mistake. I doubt we will ever turn back the clock because of the amount of money involved. Lobbyists are bribing politicians even now. It's only going to get worse. The path to legalization usually involves so-called "medical marijuana". For thousands of years, marijuana has been used for medicinal purposes, both for the quick psychological effects and as a pain medication. In Colorado, you can get a medical card that will help to avoid most of the state taxes on marijuana, which can be as high as 27%. With the card it's only about 2.9%. The trouble is 90% of the people using the medical card say they have pain. Having been a neurosurgeon for 45 years, I can tell you about 80% of the time pain is due to stress in our life, and you can't demonstrate anything medically wrong. So, to say that you have pain, which seems real to you (but is possibly made up as a reason to get a medical card) could be the gateway to a huge fraud. Many of the products are resold and sent out-of-state. Besides, we risk harming our children with real brain damage. "What's the level of your pain from 0-10?" "Well, I'm a nine, so give me a medical card." You get the point?

When William J, Bennett was the drug czar, he was able to reduce the marijuana addiction rate to 3.9% in this country, which was a tremendous achievement, considering it's now 9% in adults. He did it through extensive education of the public.

But now a number of states, including California, Colorado, Washington (the state), and Washington DC have approved the use and sale of marijuana products. All states have experienced increased healthcare costs because of it, including increased accidents and increases in school drop-out rates. The amount of money these states have received from taxation has only been about 0.1 percent of the state budget. The healthcare costs for marijuana complications were much higher than that. So increased tax money available for the state will not happen.

National statistics reveal from the year 2006 to 2010 18% of children were smoking tobacco, while 23% where are using marijuana. Twenty-three states use medical marijuana in some form or another. It is highly regulated in the state of New York. Researchers have now found that there are 33 chemicals in marijuana that can cause cancer. Smoking marijuana, which is the most common method, causes a great deal of tar in the lungs, because filters are seldom used. Marijuana smoke also goes much deeper into the lungs because it is more acidic. Incidentally, that's why there is sugar in cigarettes. It makes the smoke more acidic so nicotine can enter the blood stream more quickly. I never met a doctor who knew that. (You can find a great chapter on this topic in Gary Taub's latest book on sugar.)

Joe Califono, another health secretary at the federal level, wrote a book called *How to Raise a Drug-Free Kid*. I recommend you read it. He states children who use marijuana have a decrease in the cannabinoid receptors in the brain, and therefore have to increase the dose to get the high they're looking for. That's called tolerance, which occurs in all drug users. You see it even in people who use a lot of sugar in their food, which partly accounts for the obesity epidemic. When I tell a child that smoking marijuana may give them a pot belly, and that the girls (or boys) might not look at them, much less talk to them, they seem to pay more attention. Don't you wonder why they call it a "pot" belly?

The marijuana shops in Colorado provide customers with many different products, from candy bars, food, inhalers, reefers, etc. The main difference is in THC content. Some products go as high as 37%. Can you imagine what that might do to some people?

Let's face it, we're engaging in public policy malpractice with THC, a drug that was never properly tested by the FDA. We even have a "Grass Law," for goods generally regarded as safe. Certainly, marijuana would not qualify because of its many harmful effects. We are harming and killing our children and many adults. If the child is not addicted by age 21, the addiction rate is much less, although a lot of the side effects certainly continue: the pot bellies, the increased rates of about 20 chronic diseases, including Type II Diabetes, increase accidents, lack of ambition, etc.

The nation of Uruguay is the only other country that has allowed complete legalization. Even in the Netherlands where they have coffee shops where they sell a certain amount, it is not totally legal. What they have instead is tolerance of it. A lot of people come from other countries to buy it. As you would expect, they've had complications because of it. They now have four children's rehab centers for marijuana addiction. They are regretting what they did.

When they try to legalize marijuana in your state, they will say there is an absolute need for medical marijuana. It's a complete myth. The definition of pain is wrong. Eighty percent of the people with pain, you can tell why they hurt. To give them a quick fix like opioids for marijuana will result in addiction in a large percentage of cases. I know because as a neurosurgeon I lived in that world for decades, resulting in my writing three books on chronic pain. They are on Amazon. One has the title, *We Need a New Definition for Pain.*

In Arizona, 34,000 people use medical marijuana, and 90% say it's for pain. Pretty soon we will have a nation of pain people, with very few working, and with everyone using the medical marijuana card every day of the week.

Can you imagine the effect on our children? Incidentally, one-third of the children get their marijuana from other people's prescriptions.

In Colorado, 7.7% of the children use marijuana. Nationally, it's about 7% starting by the 12th grade. About 31.2% of people in Colorado use marijuana, higher than the 22% in the US generally. About 3000 traffic deaths occur from marijuana in the US every year. It is especially lethal when marijuana is mixed with alcohol.

In Denver, there are now more marijuana shops than Starbucks. In Los Angeles, the capital of homelessness, there are more marijuana shops than Starbucks and McDonalds combined. Incidentally, one dollar spent on teaching prevention saves generally about $10 on treatment cost.

Sanjay Gupta of CNN, who says he's a doctor, keeps on repeating anecdotal evidence on the benefits of medical marijuana. I saw his show again last Sunday and I'm very disappointed. I think he could've provided all of us with the scientific evidence of marijuana use and saved many lives. The anecdotes he brings up are not a scientific study. He is promoting the use of marijuana instead of explaining the science to the general public. He will end up harming and killing a lot of children and adults as a result of his tainted information. I would like to ask him if he is receiving some reimbursement from the industry?

The big marijuana companies depend on 20% of the population who uses. So, they need to create a lot of addicts to make their money. When these companies and legislators try to introduce marijuana to your state, they will not bring the facts because children and adults don't matter to them. They'll be speaking about medical marijuana and its unproven benefits. So, watch out and get out and vote. Falsehoods and fake news will be spread by interest groups. The political debates are about the same on the Republican and Democratic side. They all like the lobbying money.

They will falsely promote the tax benefits that have already accrued, which are non-existent. The medical calls will outpace the tax money. Legalization will cost society money, and result in injuries and deaths. Incidentally, casual use also affects the brain and the affects cannot be reversed. The science of the effects of marijuana are evolving further every day and the information is never good.

I can statistically proof that a heavy drug user started with marijuana, not opioids, 80% of the time. But what also concerns me is that the stigmatization of marijuana use is leaving us. I think CNN, by using Dr. Sanjay Gupta in their marijuana documentaries, has a lot to do with that.

We need national leadership on this issue. I'm not even thinking of political parties. Let's face it, the Obama administration did nothing to stop it and even helped promote it with a casual attitude toward marijuana use. We still don't have a drug czar in this country.

President Trump tried to appoint Senator Marino from Pennsylvania to the position, only to withdraw his nomination after an edition of 60 Minutes in January. The Senator had passed a law by consensus (no active vote) preventing the FDA from testing Class-1 drugs, including THC.

What a scam!

I even applied for the job, having written three books on opioids. I think at least I would have the passion for it. I sent my books to our governor, to Congressman Jim Banks, and the former governor of Indiana who is now Vice President.

What can I say? I'm trying.

Harming and Killing Our Children by Allowing Them to Vape

Our children are vaping cigarettes, and, yes, also marijuana. Allowing people to help themselves to nicotine in an attempt to avoid the thousands of chemicals in cigarettes is not the answer to great health for child.

The FDA announced it will give the manufacturers of electronic cigarettes 60 days to prove they can keep e-cigarettes out of the hands of children. Of course, that's an industry lobbying ploy as usual. Money talks. Do you ever feel that our democracy is actually based purely on lobbying money?

Enforcement will not be successful. Industry wins again. It's about the money honey.

The Juul brand of e-cigarettes has different flavors like crème brûlée or cucumber to make them even more irresistible, especially to a child, whose craving for sweets is even higher than an adult's. This has been well tested by the industry. Incidentally, here is something I bet you don't know: there is sugar and cigarettes. Read Dr. Gary Taub's book *The Case against Sugar*. There is a whole chapter devoted to how the industry uses sugar to make cigarettes more addictive. Sugar is what makes the smoke more acidic and opens the alveoli to allow nicotine into the bloodstream. The industry figured that out around 1920 and doubled cigarette sales.

Children are vaping at an increasing rate, especially because of the availability of medical marijuana. The experience in Colorado has not been good. In Indiana, e-cigarettes are now the main source of nicotine among the Indiana youth; 19.7% of Indiana high school students use these cigarettes on a regular basis. Even a higher percentage are smoking marijuana products.

The American Academy of Pediatrics warns that "Juuling" of cigarettes increases addiction, and yet its popularity is booming.

CNBC reported in July that e-cigarette sales have increased 800% in a recent four-week interval this year. Let's face it, if you have one addiction, odds are you will probably have another soon, be it alcohol, marijuana, cigarettes, or sugary food. The Surgeon General of United States has said the addictive potential of e-cigarettes is quite high, and we all know the use of nicotine is very unsafe, especially for children because of their undeveloped brains.

The tobacco industry tried—but fortunately failed—in its effort to win support for e-cigarettes at the World Health Conference in Geneva. Over 137 countries met at the conference in Geneva, Switzerland. The delegates were there for an update on world health related specifically to tobacco. Years ago, the group even formed a treaty to try to control the mental aspect of tobacco and nicotine addiction. A lot of their efforts were somewhat successful, according to reports. But I wondered about that the last time I traveled to Amsterdam. I thought all the people on the street were smoking. Cigarettes and marijuana are sold in their coffee shops. While walking someone rode his bike past me very fast, with a cigarette in his mouth, texting, and no hands on the handlebars. I sure can't ride a bike that well.

Industry has been searching for alternatives to combustible cigarettes because sales are down. Among the devices being considered are e-cigarettes, through which the user inhales flavored nicotine vapors. These chemicals are heated by devices which warm tobacco in a way that supposedly doesn't release carcinogens. Then again, the FDA has not tested these devices for safety. The Juul product is a flash drive look-alike whose popularity has been growing rapidly in America, especially the secondary schools.

Kids are thought to be safer than they would be using traditional cigarettes because they do not get the toxic smoke that comes from tobacco. But little is known about the health effects of all the chemicals they do inhale. Also, there is concern that non-smokers think it's less risky. They could be creating a new generation the smokers. Eventually, they become addicted to the nicotine, that tolerance is increased, maybe setting them on a path to addiction.

Talk to your kids. Don't make a friend out of them. Make them a friend after age 25. Also, of course, set a good example. Two years ago, I visited an elegant couple during a trip to see my cousin. I could not stand to be in that house because the smell of smoke was everywhere. I received a phone call a month ago from my non-smoking cousin that the beautiful couple next door we're both dead from lung cancer.

What about the Placebo Effect?

I believe that most people perceive the placebo effect as involving a medication that has no inherent value, but because the patient thinks it works, you can have an effect. In fact, a placebo can come in many forms, including people like a doctor or a healthcare provider. Sometimes, all it takes to feel better is to talk to someone who you believe can make you feel better.

Could CBD products have a placebo effect on you? If you think the product diminished your pain, there is actually a 70% chance that thinking so is what led to the reduction. Your brain and gut release dopamine and serotonin because of your positive thinking, and you say, "My pain is gone." So, when testing the effectiveness of a pill or a product from a plant, researchers must compare the results to what they get from a trial with placebos.

You won't find a single placebo-controlled study of cannabinoid products. The FDA requires these controls before approving pharmaceuticals. In this country, you cannot market placebo pills as a pharmaceutical (though it is perfectly legal in Europe). I suspect the pharmaceutical industry in this country had something to do with that.

The opposite of placebo is "nocebo," which means belief in harmful effects may lead to real harm. I wrote a book called *Nocebo: Placebos Evil Twin*.

One of the implications of the nocebo effect is that after undergoing a test like an X-ray, MRI scan, or angiogram, and being told that if you don't have some operation, injection, or pill you will be harmed, you may actually be harmed regardless of whether or not you have any real medical condition.

So, perception is extremely important. Just saying, "It cured me" does not guarantee that the product actually worked. You might just say that doesn't matter; it made me well. The trouble is when you're taking a plant product, with unpredictable and unreliable content, that also deactivates part of the main metabolizer of supplements and pharmaceuticals. Major complications, including death, could occur. If you read the references I've included in this book, you will see that it verifies what I'm saying, especially the report of Dr. Sheila Arnold from the Indiana Toxicology Department.

The relationship between the healer and the patient is huge. Someone might say to you, "It helped me a lot; it will help you," and that alone will have a great influence on how you feel. But, even if you feel better, that does not prove the product worked. It could be the power of positive thinking, "the placebo," causing real chemical changes in your body through neurotransmitters like dopamine and serotonin.

The personality and conviction of the physician, the hopeful attitude of the patient, and a positive therapeutic relationship between the two of them all work together to create positive effects. So, anecdotal reports about CBD products making people feel better are not enough. The CBD product may impact your body through positive thinking but remember these are not harmless chemicals—they affect your ability to metabolize other chemicals.

The more severe the symptoms, the worse the pain, the more likely a placebo or nocebo will work. Both expectation and emotional state can increase the likelihood of a placebo or nocebo effect.

Worry, anxiety, stress, anger, and depression negatively influence health outcomes. Cynicism, suspicion, and any pessimistic expectation can generate negative outcomes such as illness and disease. Making too much out of the symptoms that may actually need very little may lead to unnecessary surgery or medications and affect the patient's expectations.

WHAT ABOUT THE PLACEBO EFFECT?

What I am trying to say is that just because the cannabinoid product makes you feel better is not proof that it is the CBD doing it. It may be your thought process. This is based on the science behind your own feel-good neurotransmitters, dopamine and serotonin. It could also be partly the product itself, through its effect on the CB1 or CB2 receptors in your body being stimulated by your own endocannabinoids, or the in activation of the FAAS enzyme that degrades our own natural feel-good chemicals. It's the loss of the Cytochrome P450 metabolism enzymes, which degrade or inactivate the pharmaceuticals you may be taking, that worries me, as mentioned many times before.

State and Local Laws Regarding Medical Marijuana

Twenty-three states and the District of Columbia have some sort of legalized medical and/or recreational cannabis. Some of those states have limited, CBD-only laws. Eleven other states were in the process of enacting, or were likely to enact, medical and/or recreational cannabis laws by November 2016. So most of this has already happened.

The founding idea behind the state law is that medical cannabis would be used as an adjunct to other standard treatments for the specific qualifying condition. Because of the severity of the debilitating conditions of patients who qualify for medical cannabis, many of them would require a medical caregiver to help them grow or obtain cannabis plant material. What the legislators of course did not understand is that definitions of pain are extremely imprecise, making the law easy to abuse. In Colorado, people can apply for a medical marijuana pain card, which eliminates most of the tax. Also, they can say I hurt, perhaps citing a number on a 0-10 scale, and now they have medical marijuana in their hands. Can you imagine the abuse of that system?

What these legislators did is create a medical practice dictated by a political agenda rather than research. There's very little high-quality evidence to support any of the qualifying conditions in the various states' legislation. In Indiana now, anybody can buy CBD for any reason at all.

The qualifying conditions vary some from state to state and are often based on anecdotal experiences or emotional outcries from very vociferous people. But there's a lack of solid scientific research. In time, the state's specific qualifying conditions will no doubt be amended and expanded. This of course will be very unreliable because politics and lobbyists' money are involved. Because of the distinct possibility that medical cannabis will be removed from schedule 1 and designated as a schedule 2 drug in the future, the states' list of qualified conditions will probably become irrelevant in clinical practices. Remember, selling CBD in the state of Indiana at this time requires no qualifying conditions. You just buy it and use it. No educated medical provider is needed. Probably 99.9% of the buyers have no idea that CBD oils and other products can interfere with their metabolism or interact with other medications they are taking. The result can be harmful and even deadly at times.

The website www.medicalmarijuana.procon.org provides up-to-date details on the status of each state that has legalized medical cannabis. The website also maintains a current state-by-state list of approved or qualifying medical conditions and information about patient registration requirement and fees.

Additionally, each state medical board maintains this information. Its states list of qualifying medical conditions is constantly subject to change for the states. In general, the medical board for each state or jurisdiction where medical cannabis is legal has a policy statement outlining standards of good practice. In addition, each state law provides for protection of clinicians from criminal or civil liability for recommending or approving the medical use of cannabis by patients if there is a bona fide physician-patient relationship. Clinicians are allowed to openly discuss the medical use of cannabis with patient coalitions that provide cannabis to patients or direct patients where to procure cannabis. I know of some physicians who sell CBD products through a pyramid system, which allows them to make a lot of money. I don't think Indiana law protects them, no less the patient who's consuming the product.

Only Montana and Oregon allow out-of-state patients to obtain medical cannabis. Then again, if you go to Denver, there are more outlets selling marijuana products than Starbucks. Over half of the customers are out-of-state. I'm trying to paint you the real picture of what will happen in Indiana if we start allowing medical marijuana. And selling CBD oil is no better.

Most states do not have a training or continuing medical education requirement prior to recommending medical cannabis. Alaska for example has no specific training required. Arizona has developed a free 5-hour online CME course on the physician's role and expectations under the Arizona medical marijuana program. However, this is not a requirement. In California, no specific training is required, although the University of California at San Francisco has robust educational and CME offerings. In Colorado, there are no specific training or CME requirements, but the Colorado medical board is currently considering drafting a policy on the use of cannabis as a therapeutic option. Denver is trying to get this system under some control, but I won't hold my breath till they do it. In Massachusetts, physicians who certify patients for medical cannabis must first complete the Massachusetts Medical Society's online CME course on the clinical and legal aspects of the state medical cannabis law. In Michigan, no specific training or CME testing is required.

As I already mentioned, cannabis products may be of some help with chronic pain problems, the nausea and vomiting of cancer therapy, and the spasticity of multiple sclerosis. That's not a big window for therapeutic success. To me, that's not worth the risk of exposing patients to out-of-state marijuana. I'd like to think we are a lot smarter than that, in spite of our surrounding states who will probably eventually legalize marijuana.

Cannabinoid products have *not* been found significantly helpful for arthritis, glaucoma, HIV-Aids, migraines, Parkinson disease, posttraumatic stress disorder, etc.

The most important thing to remember is that the use of these products can lead to serious side effects despite what you may have heard, for example, the CBD or marijuana has never killed anyone. Just think of the accidents, overdoses, interactions with other drugs because of an activation of the cytochrome enzymes in the liver, house fires, lung damage which may lead to cancer, spousal and child abuse—I could list another 20 bad things these drugs can do to you. Next Tuesday, I'll be going to a meeting of the Indiana State Hemp Industry Association. Don't you wonder if they will bring up how their products are metabolized in the body? I'll let you know in a later chapter that I write after the meeting.

For the many illnesses mentioned in medical marijuana laws around the country, the data from scientific studies is weak or even nonexistent. The policy is not based on science. Medicine does not work this way. In medicine, we establish the safety and effectiveness of treatments *before* we recommend them to large numbers of people. It is also disturbing to think that some patients may be relying on medical marijuana when better, potentially life-saving alternatives exist. Let's face it, there are other medicines available for the three conditions.

Due to the lack of clinical trials or the inconclusive or negative results of the studies that have been completed, few major medical authorizations endorsed the use of medical marijuana. The American Medical Association, the American Psychiatric Association, the American Academy of Addiction Psychiatry, the American Society of Addiction Medicine, and the American Academy of Child and Adolescent Psychiatry have all released position papers outlining why they do not support medical marijuana. Medical marijuana laws challenge physicians to recommend use of a schedule 1 drug of abuse with no scientific approval, dosage control, or quality control. This standard recommendation is that medical marijuana should not be smoked. The main reason for this is that smoking harms our lungs and is not a safe way to take a medicine. Smoking or vaping are ways for people to feel the effects more quickly, just as some choose to inject drugs for nearly instantaneous effect.

Research examining the effects of cannabinoids may eventually make medical marijuana more feasible. Possibly, they could be made in the laboratory, so safety testing would be a lot easier. Some might say that the use of medical marijuana would prevent the use of opioids for chronic pain. Double-blind and placebo studies have not been done. So, the science is not there to prove that, only anecdotal reports.

The main reason I am against medical marijuana is that I'm concerned about increased access to marijuana, especially for young people. That is what is actually occurring in California and Colorado. The governor of the state of Colorado as a matter of fact has said, "Politics aside, I'll speak the truth, it was a major mistake to legalize marijuana in Colorado. The money we are collecting through taxes is less than the legal and medical costs."

The morality of using marijuana is another argument: many Americans simply think that marijuana is bad and that no one should ever use it. They don't care if the purpose of marijuana is medicinal or recreational. They realize too that the medical benefits are extremely minimal except for very rare seizure disorders in children.

Millions were in favor of medical marijuana on November 2012, when 63% of Massachusetts residents voted in favor of the medical marijuana. Before the vote, advertisements in support of medical marijuana told of the importance of making medical marijuana accessible to those with medical illnesses. Most of that was completely fictional and put there by industry. So, look for that to happen in Indiana. Also, keep in mind that access to marijuana will be easier, stronger, and cheaper. Marijuana will be everywhere. Recreational users prefer a stronger, and higher-grade marijuana, so they've endorsed laws that would encourage further improvement on marijuana's quantity and potency. An ounce of high-grade marijuana cost around $400 in Massachusetts, and an ounce of some high-grade marijuana in Colorado costs now around $150.

Our governor and senators and representatives unlocked the door to marijuana, approving the sale of CBD almost anywhere. Probably next year they will swing the door wide open with the approval of medical marijuana, which will benefit very few people and harm a lot. I recommend highly that you learn as much as you can about how cannabinoids are metabolized. Then you will know the real science.

The Colorado Experience

Colorado legalized medical marijuana from 2001 to 2009. The commercialized medical marijuana paved the way from 2010 till 2013 and the current status of recreational marijuana, as of 2016, as legal.

Reviewing this story, efforts, successes, and failures could be of great value for us, possibly helping us to avoid the problems while taking advantage of any successes.

The Rocky Mountain Poison and Drug Center data (RMPDC) provides medical information to healthcare providers and the public to reduce toxicity, injury, and disease related to chemical exposures of all kinds. They have been doing this for Colorado and surrounding states for over 50 years. They participate in the National Poison Data System (PDS) a pharmaceutical and medical institution for research, education, and prevention initiatives in Colorado and throughout the nation. Let's face it, this is a very good source for the information I'm going to provide for you. The Indiana State Legislature, governor, and public needs this information desperately.

Researchers have reviewed the data from emergency room visits, autopsy findings, poison control phone calls, addiction rates, etc.

I will review some of the key findings. Strong evidence shows that daily or near daily marijuana users are more likely to have impaired memory lasting a week or more after quitting. An important acute effect of THC, the primary psychoactive component of marijuana, is psychotic symptoms, such as hallucinations, paranoia, delusional beliefs, and feeling emotionally unresponsive during intoxication. The symptoms are worse with higher doses. Furthermore, daily or near daily marijuana use is associated with developing psychotic disorders such as schizophrenia. Also, marijuana users can develop cannabis use disorder, addiction, and daily or near daily marijuana users can experience withdrawal symptoms when abstaining from the drug. Evidence also shows that there are treatments for marijuana addiction that can reduce use and dependence.

Just as Dr. William Bennett had great success in reducing the opiate addiction rate in our country through public education, the Colorado RMPDC campaign of public education concerning the potential cognitive and mental health effects of marijuana use was critical. The researchers thought the public should be told the potential risks associated with daily or near daily use and abuse of potent marijuana. They also thought we should propagate accurate information about cannabis use disorder. Also, the public should know about the availability and access to treatment for cannabis use disorder.

They found substantial evidence that daily or near daily marijuana smoking is associated with chronic bronchitis, including chronic cough, sputum production, and wheezing.

They found biological evidence that THC is passed through the placentas of women who use marijuana during pregnancy and that the fetus absorbs and metabolizes the THC and passes the metabolites into the meconium. They found limited evidence that maternal use of marijuana during pregnancy is associated with an increased risk of stillbirth. They found mixed evidence for whether or not maternal use of marijuana during pregnancy is associated with birth defects, along with limited evidence that maternal use of marijuana during pregnancy is associated with isolated, simple ventricular septal defect of the heart.

They found mixed evidence for whether or not maternal use of marijuana during pregnancy is associated with decreased birth weight.

They found moderate evidence that maternal use of marijuana during pregnancy is associated with attention problems in exposed offspring. They found moderate evidence that marijuana use during pregnancy is associated with decreased IQ scores in exposed offspring, and some evidence that moderate use of marijuana during pregnancy is associated with reduced cognitive function in exposed offspring. They found moderate evidence that maternal use of marijuana during pregnancy is associated with decreased growth in exposed offspring. They found biological evidence that showed THC is present in the breastmilk of women who use marijuana. Biological evidence shows that infants who drink breastmilk containing THC absorb and metabolize the THC. They found mixed evidence for whether or not an association exists between maternal use of marijuana while breast-feeding and motor development in exposed infants.

They concluded that there is no known safe amount of marijuana use during pregnancy, that THC can pass from mother to the developing child through the placenta, that the unborn child is exposed to THC used by the mother during pregnancy, that marijuana use during pregnancy maybe associated with an increased risk of stillbirth, that marijuana use during pregnancy may be associated with an increased risk of heart defects in exposed offspring, that maternal use of marijuana during pregnancy is associated with negative effects on exposed offspring, including decreased cognitive function and inattention. These affects may not appear until adolescence. But taking marijuana during pregnancy may be associated with decreased academic ability in exposed offspring. Taking marijuana during pregnancy is associated with other negative effects on exposed offspring, including decreased growth.

In regard to the lungs, marijuana smoke may deposit more particulate matter in the lung space path compared to tobacco smoke. Daily or near daily marijuana smoking may be associated with a specific type of lung damage called bullous lung disease, resulting in a collapsed lung, in individuals younger than 40 years of age.

The researchers mentioned that marijuana vaping is increasing in popularity, as is occurring in Fort Wayne, and the public believes vaporizing marijuana to be less harmful or healthier than smoking marijuana.

Unfortunately, the science will take a little bit of time to come to a definite conclusion.

The researchers felt an educational program for pregnant women, their families, and healthcare providers who care for pregnant women is needed to ensure that more information is shared about the known health effects, and also about what is unknown at present.

Colorado politicians ignored major pot problems according to *The Colorado Springs Gazette* editorial board, writing in 2018. It's no different in Indiana. They allowed the public to use CBD oil without informing them of possible interactions with the medications they are already taking.

Gov. John Hickenlooper said, "It's not a black market anymore. It's not a criminal activity, and we would hate for the state to go backwards," expressing concern about the potential for more federal enforcement against his state's legal marijuana industry. They felt they had the state's right to sanction, host, and profit from an industry that frequently violates federal law to the detriment of traffic safety, federal lands, children, and neighboring states that are bombarded with Colorado pot. I feel Colorado politicians need to stop pandering and instead start leading, which means telling the truth about the severely negative consequences a big commercial pot. The governor and other politicians tell us everything is rosy, but that's not what we are hearing from educators, cops, social workers, doctors, drug counselors, parents, and others in the trenches of the world's first anything-goes marijuana free-for-all. It's not what they are seeing in the streets. If the government wants to lead on this issue, they would be telling the world about their rate of homelessness, which all major homeless shelter operators attribute to commercialized, recreational pot.

Honestly, they would talk about illegal growing operations invading neighborhoods and public lands. They would stop selling positive impressions about a failed policy for the sake of appearing to respect the will of voters. They would not bow to public perception but would guide it in a new direction. Let this be a lesson for the people and politicians in Indiana.

THE COLORADO EXPERIENCE

The government says legalization has eliminated illegal pot in Colorado. People who enforce the law consider that laughable. Mayor John Suthers, Colorado's former US Attorney, speaks of hundreds of illegal pot operations in Colorado Springs he hopes to raid. Leading law enforcers describe illegal productivity that exceeds limits of departmental budgets and personnel.

A massive black market has been attracted to federal property. Major Mexican cartels have developed growth operations west of Colorado Springs. There have been 17 arrests of cartel operations in the past 18 months. These used to be in Mexico, before legalization made Colorado more attractive. Colorado lacks the resources to make a dent in the additional cartel activity in the regions two national forests. The black market invading Colorado's national forests is growing so large the entire budget for San Isabel Forest would not cover the cost of removing and mediating cartel growing operations in the forest, a government official said. Most of this information comes from the *Colorado Springs Gazette*. The editors also say, "No black market, no crimes? Tell that to the cartels. They come to a marijuana land in the wake of Amendment 64, wisely betting state leaders will defend their risky and unprecedented allotment. They count on politicians to look the other way, so they can tell the world the new system works."

Let's review a few other statistics from Colorado. Emergency room visits have increased, and hospitalizations with marijuana-related billing codes have significantly increased. Rates of hospitalization for children under nine years of age and emergency room visits related to poisoning possibly due to marijuana have likewise increased significantly.

We have to congratulate Colorado public health for stepping up to bat and making their data available to everyone in the world. Personally, I'd like to see more data regarding the effects of CBD and marijuana on the people who are taking supplements and pharmaceuticals. Data is clearly available, but the more the better.

What the Indiana legislature Could Learn from Colorado, California, Oregon and the State of Washington

In 1969, just 2% of Americans thought marijuana legalization was a good idea. By 2005, only about one-third of Americans supported legalization. Sadly, legalization is no longer a minority position. Now that you have some knowledge of the science of the effects of cannabinoids on society and our health, you'll understand why this concerns me. Unfortunately, about the same number of Democrats, Republicans, and Independents support legalization of marijuana products. Frankly, that tells us it will be difficult to overcome the lobbyists. You and I know it's about the money.

Have you noticed that former politicians are joining the boards of cannabinoid companies? Paul Ryan would be an example. The head of the Indiana Senate resigned his job on November 6 and is joining a lobbying company in Indianapolis. I wonder whether they will be lobbying for or against some of these companies. Take your guess. After all, David Long was in charge of the Senate when they passed the new CBD Law. I did not read anything in the paper saying that he disagreed with that.

CBD OIL: INDIANA'S ROAD TO MARIJUANA

The first step on the road to legalization of marijuana has started in most states with so-called "medical marijuana." I understand that this subject will come up in next year's session of the Indiana Legislature. My dream is that they have a copy of this book in the office of every Senator and Representative so that they may be a little bit more informed of the science of cannabinoids. I'm trying to do what I can, because I'm a doctor. Legalization advocates cleverly and cynically promote marijuana as a last resort for patients suffering from cancer, HIV, multiple sclerosis, glaucoma, and numerous other maladies. As I reviewed in other chapters, The National Academies of Science, Engineering, and Medicine have stated that medicinal marijuana has been found to be helpful for the treatment of chronic pain, the nausea and vomiting associated with cancer, and the spasticity of multiple sclerosis, with very little discussion of the dangers of CBD and marijuana, essentially ignoring that the cannabinoids have an effect on Cytochrome P450 that can cause serious complications and possibly even death.

Anecdotal testimony is not science, but it has appealed to the public's natural desire to help those in pain and persuaded many that marijuana does have a useful purpose in society. Numerous states, either by legislative action or referendum, created "medical marijuana" programs. Although they were initially designed to provide marijuana to a limited group of patients, in many places this ultimately expanded into actual or de facto recreational use programs with widespread abuse. Some states have more closely regulated structures in place, and the numbers of dispensaries are limited in those locations. However, no doctor in any program actually prescribes marijuana, as is done with every other drug requiring a physician's authorization.

Further, in most states, a doctor gives the patient a note or letter that permits that person to obtain a medical marijuana card. In states like California and Colorado, well over 90% of cardholder's licenses simply list "My level of pain is a ten" as the ailment for which they need the marijuana. The overwhelming majority of these cardholders are males under the age of 35. Do you imagine there could be some fraud going on here? There is no way to verify the level of a person's pain. Much of the purchased "medical marijuana" finds its way into the hands of children and adolescents. Most medicines the

WHAT THE INDIANA LEGISLATURE COULD LEARN FROM COLORADO, CALIFORNIA, OREGON AND THE STATE OF WASHINGTON

FDA requires to be safe and effective, but marijuana is unregulated, non-standardized, and is proving to be either unsafe or ineffective. Furthermore, because medical marijuana is not regulated, dosage is inconsistent, and purity is unknown.

For children who have a very unusual seizure condition, the doctor can now write a prescription for an FDA-approved CBD product, the plant-derived drug called Epidiolox. We don't need to legalize marijuana so a child might be prescribed a drug that might help them. Those seizure conditions are extremely rare.

Knowing what we know about marijuana today, and all the attending problems that come with it, including many worse than those caused by tobacco—permanent impairment of the brain in adolescents, for example—I find it incredible that the move to legalize marijuana has become so mainstream. At least 23 states and the District of Columbia have done it. Colorado, Washington, Oregon, Alaska, and Washington DC have fully legalized a drug for recreational use that is not of any use whatsoever.

Uruguay, Canada, and the US are leading the world in the legalization of marijuana products. The recent election may have added a few states that will change their legal status (but I've heard nothing about it in the news so far). My wife tells me she heard on the late news that part of the reason that Attorney General Jeff sessions lost his job was because he was holding up marijuana legislation. Of course, that concerns me a great deal. I suspect lobbying and campaign money are speaking here.

Adding marijuana to the list of legal products will do little if anything to diminish the dangers or use of alcohol and will instead lead to yet more social and economic chaos. I'm mostly concerned of course about the lack of discussion about how cannabinoids are metabolized. I'm afraid that story is yet to be written. Then again, I am doing my best.

I encourage you to read *Going to Pot* by William J. Bennett. I quote from it liberally. It clearly states.

- Marijuana is not safe

- Marijuana is, except in very few cases, not medicinal
- Other countries that have experimented with decriminalization are now trying to reverse such experiments
- Already, American localities that have experimented with legalization of marijuana laws are regretting it
- There is no logical argument on behalf of states' rights to decide for themselves how to regulate marijuana—it is not a fundamental right
- Marijuana can be addictive
- Marijuana use can be a gateway to abuse of other drugs
- Marijuana is particularly harmful to, and addictive for, teenagers
- We can reduce use and abuse of dangerous substances in America, just as we have before

I would like to complement William J. Bennett, as he was America's first drug czar under President George H.W. Bush. In this position, he was able to cut drug use and addiction rates to alcohol and opioids through public education in schools, newspapers, the internet, and television. It had a major effect on our nation. We all should be thankful for that. But it also tells us it could be done again.

Two False Beliefs

A significant number of people believe that marijuana is not addictive and does not cause withdrawal. It has been statistically proven that 9% of adults who smoke marijuana daily or at least every other day eventually become addicted. About 17% of children who smoke marijuana regularly become addicted to it and will experience the negative effects more profoundly because the brain is not fully developed till around age 25. I will include in this book a few chapters on the effects of marijuana on children.

When people who are smoking marijuana daily or nearly every day try to stop smoking, they experience withdrawal symptoms. These include anxiety, irritability, and trouble sleeping. While some people debate whether marijuana is harmful or whether marijuana is addictive, withdrawal does not seem to be on the radar. Most people have not even thought about whether stopping marijuana use causes withdrawal symptoms.

Actually, there is a Marijuana Withdrawal Syndrome in the scientific literature. The American Psychiatric Association added Marijuana Withdrawal Syndrome to the recent edition of its guidebook on psychiatric classifications, the DSM5. Studies have demonstrated that marijuana withdrawal symptoms are very similar to nicotine withdrawal symptoms. Anyone who thinks that stopping cigarette smoking is easy is living in a dream world.

The syndrome occurs after someone stops using marijuana after having used it heavily for an extended period of time. Overall, nicotine and marijuana withdrawal cause similar symptoms: people feel lousy and their cravings often result and continued use of marijuana or tobacco and a lot of the time both.

Smoking marijuana daily or nearly every day is called, "Using heavily." Using four days a week is called "Regular use." Most marijuana smokers do it multiple times a day, just like cigarettes. The pattern of using a lot of marijuana may be influenced by the illegal status of marijuana in mostly nice states that limits its availability.

Marijuana withdrawal symptoms begin within a few days of stopping heavy marijuana use. Symptoms can include anger, feelings of aggression, depressed mood, and loss of appetite. Remember that marijuana causes the munchies in many people. They can develop a "pot belly." So, when they stop, generally the appetite decreases. That is tightly controlled by the CB1 receptor in the hypothalamus. Physical symptoms of withdrawal may include headaches, stomach pains, increased sweating, fever, chills, or shakiness. These withdrawal symptoms are severe enough to interfere with the person's functioning at work or in social situations.

Many of us are familiar with how difficult it can be to stop smoking cigarettes and, more recently, we discovered how difficult it is to stop using opiates like oxycodone or heroin. Thinking of marijuana withdrawal as being similar to nicotine withdrawal is helpful. You know that when people quit smoking, nicotine withdrawal makes them extremely irritable and anxious. Also, after a while, they start gaining weight again. This is because the receptors never used by cigarettes or marijuana are now being satisfied by sugar. Obesity is the result. During withdrawal, they don't want to be around other people, and most people don't want to be around them for fear of receiving their wrath or abuse. When trying to quit, it is very difficult to concentrate. It is also a challenge to be engaged in family or social activities. Those trying to quit nicotine constantly fight the urge to give in and smoke. Quitting marijuana is the same way. This is another example of how marijuana is so much like other drugs that we recognize as addictive and difficult to quit. A physician like myself, knowing that, I take advantage of it and give the patient some advice on how to deal with an addiction. These withdrawal symptoms make you feel absolutely miserable, often leading to relapse, just as nicotine withdrawal can lead to a relapse in cigarette use, or opioid withdrawal.

People who smoke marijuana many times don't understand that stopping it came be difficult, and they do not expect withdrawal symptoms.

And, talking with patients with marijuana addiction who have had multiple failed attempts to quit, I know this is a common theme. They were not aware of the physical withdrawal symptoms they would experience and were ill-prepared to deal with feeling terrible, anxious and physically sick. Patients often describe a sense of relief when they learn about the marijuana withdrawal syndrome, as it validates their difficulties in stopping the use of marijuana. The withdrawal syndrome provides a conceptual framework that can help them understand why they have found it so difficult to stop using a drug good of friends say is not addictive. Educating a patient about the signs of marijuana addiction can be great way to jump start treatment, or not to start smoking it in the first place. Public education is critical. When I hear from children that about 30% of the students are smoking marijuana at the college level, and that 20% are already smoking at the high school level, I wonder what our educational system and the government are doing?

The second myth is that marijuana use cannot lead to addiction. Even many physicians believe that. Many people and medical providers are just frankly uninformed. Maybe that includes our legislature and governor, or maybe they're just more motivated by the lobbyists from the industry. I am quoting liberally from a book written by Dr. Kevin P. Hill, MD, who is an addiction psychiatrist who conducts research in hopes of finding a medication to treat marijuana addiction. It is quite clear after reading his book that marijuana addiction is real for sure. When he found and heard that other doctors were saying that they thought marijuana was not addictive, he was surprised. He came to realize that these doctors were simply reflecting a common myth about marijuana. He states that marijuana is potentially addictive; 9% of adults and 70% of adolescents who use marijuana developed an addiction, resulting in 2.7 million Americans meeting the criteria today for marijuana addiction. Causing addictions usually means causing harm, so understanding how marijuana use can lead to marijuana addiction in some people is important because the first marijuana myth—"Marijuana is not harmful." The signs, however, suggest that while marijuana is considered "a soft drug" by many, it has much in common with hard drugs known for their addictive qualities.

Addiction is a chronic medical illness like asthma, diabetes, or high blood pressure. These chronic medical illnesses have a genetic component, which explains why you are at higher risk for having addiction problems if someone in your family struggles with addiction, compared with someone with no family history of addiction. But genes don't determine destiny 90% of the time.

One study conducted in 2007 showed that genetic factors account for 35% of heritability of marijuana addiction, and environmental factors account for 47%. The neighborhood you live in also clearly affects the rate of marijuana use in adults and children.

The genes for addiction seem to have a strong pull, affecting many choices people make in behaviors. Making bad decisions is often due to impulsivity, stress in the family, and the person's tendency to make quick decisions before thanking them through.

Being under the influence of substances makes it more likely that you will make an impulsive decision that you might not otherwise make. Most of the chemicals people used to get intoxicated or high have a side effect of relaxing judgment, making us vulnerable to poor or impulsive decision-making. Morality may be thrown out of the window.

Environmental factors, such as once daily social interactions, play a role in the development of addiction. For example, living in close proximity to family members or friends struggling with addiction makes it more difficult for someone with a genetic predisposition to addiction to stay away from the drugs. Those with a history of addiction have a high level of sensitivity to signals. This is called cue reactivity. A person with a history of alcoholism for example reacts to a drink more strongly than someone without such a history.

TWO FALSE BELIEFS

Many people describe addiction as a brain disease. Addiction causes your brain to go through changes at the most basic levels, within the cells, which are building blocks of your body's organs, including the brain. You can see that the developing brain of a child could be more severely affected than that of an adult. Drug use leads to the release of brain chemicals called neurotransmitters. One of these chemicals, dopamine, affects a part of the brain called the nucleus accumbens, our pleasure center. It's the quick-fix center, which can make you feel like saying, "I'm in heaven."

The marijuana chemicals hit these pleasure receptors, which undo locks. When people use drugs over and over, this process occurs again and again, and after a while, the receptors get worn out and the body cannot produce enough new receptors to replace the old ones. As a result, what occurs is called "down regulation," the decreased production of the particular receptors associated with the drug being used. Therefore, you have developed tolerance and need to take a lot more to feel the same as you did previously after using marijuana.

Medical Marijuana

The tide is turning. Personally, I think Indiana is on the road to legalizing marijuana. This year they started with CBD. You can buy it almost anywhere, with no age restrictions for as I know, no written warnings about how it is eventually metabolized. I've included in this book a chapter about that. Be sure you read it, especially if you're considering using CBD.

I would estimate that about 60% of the people in the US favor the use of medical marijuana. The state of California was a first to enact medical marijuana laws in 1966. Since then at least 23 or more states have passed state laws implementing medical marijuana programs. The science of medical marijuana is slowly developing.

I have reviewed The National Academy of Sciences, Engineering, and Medicine's Report of 2017. They in essence reviewed the world's literature regarding the health effects of cannabis and cannabinoids.

I will review some of conclusions with you by the NASEM.

There is substantial evidence of a statistical association between cannabis use and the development of schizophrenia or other psychoses, with the highest risk among the most frequent users. There is moderate evidence of a statistical association between cannabis use and better cognitive performance among individuals with psychotic disorders with a history of cannabis use and increased symptoms of mania and hypomania in individuals diagnosed with bipolar disorders. A small increase was found for a likelihood of the development of depressive disorders, with an increased incidence of suicidal ideation and suicide attempts, with a higher incidence among heavy users. There was also an increased incidence of suicide completion, and an increased incidence of social anxiety disorder.

There is moderate evidence of a statistical association between cannabis use and impairment in the cognitive domains of learning, memory, and attention. There is substantial evidence of a statistical association between maternal cannabis smoking and lower birth weight of the offspring. There is moderate evidence of a statistical association between cannabis use an increased risk of overdose injuries among pediatric populations in the US states where cannabis is legal.

There is substantial evidence of a statistical association between cannabis use an increased risk of motor vehicle crashes. There is substantial evidence of a statistical association between cannabis smoking and respiratory symptoms and more frequent chronic bronchitis episodes.

There is conclusive or substantial evidence cannabis or cannabinoids are effective for the treatment of chronic pain in adults. They can be effective medications in the treatment of chemotherapy-induced nausea and vomiting, and also for improving patient-reported multiple sclerosis spasticity symptoms.

Treating the above three conditions can be the main benefits of using cannabinoid products.

I will write in another chapter my concerns about the definition of pain. "What's the level of your pain from 0 to 10?" doesn't do it for me. I need to know why you have the pain. In Colorado where marijuana is legalized, there has been great abuse of using pain to get medical marijuana. You can see the point.

There is insufficient evidence to support or refute the conclusion that cannabinoids are an effective treatment for the mental health outcomes in individuals with schizophrenia or schizophrenia-type psychoses.

There have been great research gaps, largely due to government restricting the research on cannabis products, which were probably promoted by the pharmaceutical industry because they cannot patent plant products. There is limited evidence that cannabidiol is an effective treatment for the improvement of anxiety symptoms.

There is insufficient evidence that cannabinoids are an effective treatment for the motor systems symptoms associated with Parkinson's disease. There's insufficient evidence that cannabinoids are an effective treatment for the symptoms associated with amyotrophic lateral sclerosis.

California was the first state to enact medical marijuana laws in 1996. Twenty-three states have followed, including the District of Columbia. The issue has been hotly debated in recent years as the topic has made its way onto the ballot in state after state. I know it was on a number of states' ballots yesterday when people went to the polls on November 6, 2018. I don't know the results yet.

Cutting edge cannabinoid research is taking place on a daily basis throughout the world, especially in Israel where it is completely legal to do so. I reviewed that, at least in part. I know it is largely driven by industry, and normally they don't report negative results, which makes it difficult for me to evaluate what they're printing. I could not find any articles on how cannabis is metabolized in the liver.

As you already know, there are two main types of cannabinol receptors, CB1 and CB2. CB1 receptors are located throughout the body, but they're concentrated heavily in the brain. CB2 receptors are located throughout the arms and legs, but they also found in the organs of the body.

The two main cannabinols, or active ingredients, of marijuana are CBD and THC. They are responsible for the effects that are typically associated with marijuana. There are many other cannabinoids, and some of them may prove to play important roles as medications or in marijuana if medicinal effects are discovered. THC can produce psychosis in a small number of people who are vulnerable to its effect. CBD is not thought to be psychoactive, but if you heat it, it can become so. It tells you how to do it on the internet.

There are three synthetic cannabinoids that are approved for unusual seizures in children. They are very rare. Another one was approved recently by the FDA, which actually comes from a plant. Again, it's for a very rare seizure disorder and requires a prescription. The latter are much safer because the medical provider can explain the potential side effects and benefits. That's not the case when you're buying the products without a prescription.

Methods of Using Medical Cannabis

The methods for consuming medical marijuana are essentially the same as using recreational marijuana. Smoking or vaping are the most common methods. The ingredients are released through heating. Vaping is about four times more common than smoking. Medical marijuana may also be ingested orally, taken as tea, juice, or in a liquid extract form.

Medical marijuana can be smoked in a pipe or joint. The cannabinol components, mainly CBD and THC, are rapidly absorbed into the lungs, then into the bloodstream, then across the blood-brain barrier to stimulate the CB1 receptors for its psychotropic effects. The effects of marijuana can therefore be felt within a few minutes, which gradually reduce after 2 to 3 hours. So, it is used for treating acute symptoms that need immediate attention. Examples would be acute pain, spasms, nausea, and vomiting. Remember, medical evidence for effectiveness is only for chronic pain, nausea, the vomiting associated with cancer treatment, and the spasticity associated with multiple sclerosis. But don't forget that marijuana also has side effects.

The disadvantage to smoking marijuana is that harmful substances in the smoke could irritate the lungs, black tar for example, leading to the possibility of developing lung cancer in the future.

Vaping is like smoking, but a vape pen or similar device is used instead. No smoke is produced because the marijuana is heated and not burned. Through heating, the active ingredients are released and then inhaled into the lungs. The effect is also instantly felt, like with smoking. Most researchers agree that vaporizing is as effective as smoking, but healthier.

Cannabis also can come in edible snacks, like cookies, brownies, and candies. Essentially, these are cooked using oil or butter infused with marijuana. The effects of orally ingested cannabis last longer than smoke or inhaled marijuana, usually between 5 to 6 hours after eating. However, the effects take longer to be felt, roughly 30 to 90 minutes after eating. Also, they have to go through something called the first pass affect, which means they are metabolized in the liver and lose 80% of their effectiveness. So, this method it is highly dependent on the ability of the liver, which will be different in almost everyone.

Cannabis tinctures, of which Green Dragon and Golden Dragon are examples, are made by dissolving marijuana in alcohol or a similar solvent. A small amount is then placed under the tongue, and you wait for it to work. The onset and duration of the effect of cannabis tinctures is similar to that of edible cannabis.

Sub-lingual sprays consist of cannabis extracts often mixed with another substance such as coconut oil. The effects are quickly felt, generally within 5 to 15 minutes. This method is therefore well-suited to the treatment of acute pain; it is quick, discreet, and smokeless.

Capsules and gel caps containing cannabis oil present another very easy method of treatment with medical marijuana. The dosing effect and duration are similar to that when ingesting edible cannabis.

Another method is using topical motions and salves. This method is suitable for treating skin conditions, pain, infections, and inflammation.

Cannabis oil extracts are made of concentrated marijuana, and they are very potent. When you heat CBD, some of it converts to THC, and so the product can therefore produce feelings of any duration if high doses are taken.

Medical Marijuana Side Effects

The side effects can include dizziness, sleepiness, short-term memory loss, euphoric feelings, or a high. In some cases, there are more serious side effects, like psychosis and severe anxiety.

You also have to remember my previous multiple warnings that cannabis as marijuana or CBD can inhibit the P450 cytochrome system to an unpredictable extent and therefore could cause great harm or even a death because of the body's resulting inability to detoxify supplements and medications the patient is already taking. I say again, this is a major problem and the industry and government are not properly warning the public.

It is important to realize that the side effects depend not just on the dosage, and the cannabis strain taken, but also on the sensitivity, race, and sex of the particular person taking the drug. A recent scientific paper concludes that the black population is affected twice as much, and women are affected much more than men. Watch out! The risk is even higher in women who are pregnant, patients with a heart problem, where there is a history of psychosis, and when the person is under 18 years of age.

Legalization of Marijuana Can Lead to Other Problems.

In 2016, the state of Colorado said that taxing marijuana only accounted for 1.18% of Colorado's total revenue from taxes.

The costs involved with law-enforcement, crime, compliance regulation, prevention and awareness campaigns, large school programs, habituation and addiction treatment services, and healthcare, not to mention people not applying for jobs or staying home because of loss of ambition, are all higher now than the tax money they are collecting. The governor said, "Let's be honest, not political, it was a mistake to legalize marijuana." Check the information online if you don't believe me.

Other complications have included increased poison control calls, increased emergency room visits, traffic fatalities involving marijuana, and increasing marijuana use by young people (74% higher than the national average). Black market demand has increased, while cheap, low quality imports have decreased, and the illegal exportation of high-quality to neighboring states has spiked dramatically. Some are using it while they're driving home, leading to major accidents with injuries and loss of life.

These early returns haven't been encouraging. It's a stretch to believe that if Indiana were to go for legalized pot things would be any different. Also, just because it could be legal in the future doesn't mean marijuana is a good idea for anybody in our state. Just call a rehab center in Colorado or California and you will get an earful. I did.

The lesson to the legislature and Governor should be that the state will probably lose money from legalization, and a lot of people will be injured, and some will die because they are already on other medications and the combination cannot be properly metabolized (Read my chapter on Cytochrome P450 metabolism.).

The Entourage Effect: Drug Interaction

Commercially available CBD oil has many cannabinoids in it, including THC, THCA, CBD, CBDA, CBN, CBG, CBC, CBL, CVV, THCV, CBDV, CBCV, CBGV, CBE, and CBT.

The Entourage Effect is a proposed mechanism by which compounds present in cannabis, which are largely non-psychoactive by themselves, modulate the overall psychoactive effects of the plant. It is the interaction of the above chemicals that is the bottom line, the true effect on the patient.

The trouble is that this has not been studied to any significant degree. You can only pull up about three controlled scientific studies on CBD.

With cannabis, not only are the dozens of cannabinoids important, but studies have shown that the plethora of terpenoids, which lend to the aroma and color of cannabinoids in the flower of marijuana, present in the cannabis plant also contribute to the entourage effect.

The effect of all these chemicals can be inhibitory or excitatory—in other words, they're unpredictable, with important possible consequences. Of course, THC and CBD are the most important and most prominent contents in the hemp plant. The amount of THC should be very low in the CBD products, 0.3%, but at this time the reports from testers are only about 26% accurate. The THC content actually may be a lot higher. So, the entourage effect could just about produce any combination to the user, making the chemicals either therapeutic or harmful and potentially deadly depending on what other medications the user is taking, a blood thinner for example, or a diabetes medication, etc.

Some people think the entourage effect helps to modulate our own endocannabinoid system, making it work better. Then again, controlled scientific studies are hard to find. The entourage effect is used in the development of cannabis-based medications. Often the medications will be shown by the ratio of CBD to THC. For example, the best tinctures for childhood seizures have a ratio of around 18 to 1. Pain is usually best treated with a 1 to 1 ratio. Then again, the companies selling a product never mention how CBD turns off some of the cytochrome enzymes. At least, I've not seen it or heard it discussed at the public meetings I've attended.

A good book that I read called *CBD* by Leonard Leinow focuses immediately on THC. It is precisely because of the entourage effect that it is so effectively therapeutic, he states. He's really saying, "It's THC that makes CBD have some effect."

"I feel great", "I can't live without it"—isn't that what people who are addicted to alcohol, cigarettes, and marijuana say? Let's be open-minded and realistic. It is the interaction of all these chemicals that has unpredictable effects on us. CBD is the most potent anti-inflammatory phytocannabinoid and is second in its effects only to THC.

Neither THC nor CBD are present in the plant in active forms until it is heated, which can be accomplished by smoking the plant, vaporizing it, or pre-cooking it in an oven before adding it to edibles or liquids, a process known as decarboxylation. A very small amount of CBD breaks down to the THC in the body, an action that may explain its side effects of drowsiness. In some patients, daytime drowsiness does occur.

The phytocannabinoid and endocannabinoid systems both exhibit the entourage effect of synergism among various components. What I've tried to tell you is that the entourage effect is another reason that using CBD products can give an unpredictable result, especially since the testing runs only about a 26% accuracy rate, according to an article in the Fort Wayne Medical Society's Bulletin.

Combining Alcohol and CBD Oil Can Be Deadly

Imagine driving down the road and you've been drinking above or below the legal limit and you have been using CBD products or maybe even medical marijuana. No one would be surprised if you're involved in an accident, injuring or killing yourself and the other people you hit. Maybe it's a school bus. Just imagine. What if there was no alcohol or CBD or marijuana?

Alcohol dependence relies on a few different metabolic pathways in the human body, with the primary enzymes involved being:

- Alcohol D hydrogenase (ADH)
- Aldehyde dehydrogenase (AL DH)
- Cytochrome P450: specifically (CYP2E1)

Usually, the first two handle the alcohol metabolism, but in all chronic alcohol consumers the CYP450 gets involved to assist with the overload.

Of interest also is that CB1 receptor agonists, like THC, encourage alcohol consumption. Although the pharmacokinetics of alcohol and CBD are not yet well understood, what we do know is that CBD inhibits the CYP450 enzyme system, and the two play a huge role in alcohol metabolism.

Appreciate a Second Opinion

I reviewed an excellent article in *Consumer Reports* by Lisa L. Gill titled "New Hope for Pain Relief?" I thought it was thorough and well-balanced.

She confirms that the FDA's approval of Epidiolex, a CBD drug derived from the sativa marijuana plant for a very rare seizures, does not establish the drugs usefulness for any other conditions.

She also states that Johns Hopkins and the University of California are studying other potential uses for cannabinoids, including CBD. The major question has been whether CBD could be used as a substitute for opioids.

Part of the problem has been that the government, possibly because of the pharmaceutical industry, has created rules that for years prevented scientists from using federal money on research into cannabinoids' possible health benefits and on how cannabinoids are metabolized by the liver. We already have that knowledge, but the scientists need to spread it around. I suspect industry has something to do with the failure up till now. The article mentions that the National Institutes of Health (NIH) awarded around $40 million toward cannabis research, with $15 million going to CBD prep studies.

Gill also reports that until evidence from this new research starts emerging, conclusive findings will be hard to come by. A researcher from

Johns Hopkins said, "Other than epilepsy, at this point, we have mostly postulation, not proof."

As I have mentioned many times, states are approving CBD to treat conditions based on anecdotal reports and preliminary data. The doctor from Johns Hopkins agrees with that. It may be a false hope, in my opinion.

The article refers to the report in 2017 by Dr. Donald Abrams, who worked on the panel for the National Academies of Science, Engineering, and Medicine, which reported that cannabinoids can be helpful for the treatment of pain, the nausea of cancer, and spasticity associated with multiple sclerosis. But the interesting thing was that they could find only three published randomized trials, the gold standard of research, that looked at just CBD, confirming my suspicion that the science supporting the use of CBD does not exist. In other words, we don't have the science to take it in the first place and are exposing ourselves to the potential harming or deadly side effects. That CBD can turn off some of the cytochrome enzymes, including P450, is strong reason against using it in the first place.

Gill does mention in her article that some research suggests CBD may interact with several kinds of prescription meds, which I speak about repeatedly because of the danger. That's why I especially like this article, because it is confirming what I am saying. Gill also says that if you wonder into the idea of taking some of the cannabinoids that you see a trained doctor who is knowledgeable about how they affect your metabolism. Let's face it, what are the odds of finding a doctor like that?

Gill also discusses the unreliability of the tests of contents of many of the products. It varies from company to company, but it's not an FDA-screened product, and it may contain a mix of more than 100 other compounds found in the cannabis plant.

Summary: The Road to Marijuana

I've tried to tell you the history of cannabis and the spread of its use across civilizations for the last few thousand years.

I've highlighted its original use in industry, for the manufacturing of everything from ropes and sails, to its use in religion and recreation. I've tried to discuss the good and the bad, the forgotten, and the hidden.

As you well know, there is a freight train coming at us. It's filled with politicians and captains of industry who have absolutely no regard for your life. I mean every word of what I've said and printed and talked about on television and radio. I would greatly appreciate anyone who might join me in trying to stop this train.

Yesterday, I again called Sheila Arnold PHD from the state toxicology department. I again invited her to come to Fort Wayne to give a lecture to the people of Fort Wayne and surrounding areas, as well as the medical providers who want to know the true science of CBD, which is being sold everywhere. I also wanted her to tell us about the toxicology of marijuana. I read in yesterday's paper that Michigan has approved recreational marijuana. We live very close to the border, and we know what's coming soon. Certainly, I'm aware it's here already but it's going to get worse.

Dr. Sheila Arnold said she was just too busy. I had first requested the lecture a few months ago. I had heard from a prosecutor at a political meeting recently that she came to Fort Wayne frequently to testify in cases he was handling. He thought it would be easy for me to meet with her. Incidentally, when I spoke with her previously, she said she'd have to check with her boss and he would have to check with the governor as to whether she could give a lecture or even possibly do a Public Access TV show. I assured her the information was critical to the health of our area.

Do you think politics may be involved here? Maybe nobody cares? I'm just looking for help to educate the public.

Briefly, the science that disturbs me includes findings like:

- The testing of the chemical contents of CBD products is only about 25% reliable.
- The entourage effect (the interaction of CBD with other chemicals in the plant) is unpredictable. There are many other cannabis chemicals in hemp.
- CBD partially deactivates Cytochrome P450, which is the body's main detoxifier of supplements and pharmaceuticals.
- Heating CBD can partially convert it into THC, the main psychoactive component of marijuana. The method is readily available online; people are already doing it.
- Smoking and vaping CBD automatically results in the conversion of some CBD to THC, while at the same time leading to the familiar bad health effects of inhaling smoke, including chronic pulmonary disease, and some addiction. Incidentally, the sugar in a lot of the vaping products increases the addiction rate.
- Businesses that sell products most of the time do not warn the customer of the potential interaction of medications they are taking, including supplements, with CBD, which can be very harmful and even deadly.

- Periodic workplace surprise blood testing for opioids and cannabinoids may cost you your job. It may take a month to clear the blood of these products.
- CBD products often contain contaminants and adulterants, unknown to you, and potentially dangerous to your health.
- Manufacturers, distributors, sellers, and testers may be legally liable if a buyer decides to sue. This was told to me by a number of attorneys.

Hopefully, I have increased your knowledge. Every day, I try to read more to increase mine. Hopefully, I can stop some people from becoming addicted, prevent them from developing the complications of drug interaction, and maybe save a few lives.

After all, I am a doctor.

References

Understanding Marijuana by Mitch Earleywine

CBD: A Patient's Guide to Medicinal Cannabis by Leonard Leinow and Juliana Birnbaum

CBD: What You Need to Know by Gregory L Smith MD

Fort Wayne Medicine Quarterly: Fall 2018, Volume 16.3

Indiana State Department of Toxicology: Sheila A. Arnold, PhD (PowerPoint)

The Health Effects of Cannabis and Cannabinoids by The National Academies of Science, Engineering, & Medicine: Report-2017

Going to Pot by William J. Bennett

Medical Cannabis by Gregory L. Smith, MD

www.projectcbd.org/article/CBD-Drug-interactions-role-cytochrome-450

Made in the USA
Columbia, SC
24 December 2018